LIFE CYCLES

The Crocodile

Diana Noonan

CHELSEA
CLUBHOUSE
An Imprint of Chelsea House Publishers
A Haights Cross Communications Company
Philadelphia

This edition first published in 2003 in the United States of America by Chelsea Clubhouse, a division of Chelsea House Publishers and a subsidiary of Haights Cross Communications.

Chelsea Clubhouse
1974 Sproul Road, Suite 400
Broomall, PA 19008-0914

The Chelsea House world wide web address is www.chelseahouse.com

Library of Congress Cataloging-in-Publication Data

Noonan, Diana.
    The crocodile / by Diana Noonan.
    p. cm. — (Life cycles)
    Summary: An introduction to the physical characteristics, behavior, and development of crocodiles, reptiles that are in danger from both animal and human predators.
    ISBN 0-7910-6964-8
    1. Crocodiles—Life cycles—Juvenile literature. [1. Crocodiles. 2. Endangered species.] I. Title. II. Series.
    QL666.C925 N66 2003
    597.98'2—dc21

                                                                                    2002000035

First published in 1999 by
MACMILLAN EDUCATION AUSTRALIA PTY LTD
627 Chapel Street, South Yarra, Australia, 3141

Copyright © Diana Noonan 1999
Copyright in photographs © individual photographers as credited

Edited by Anne McKenna
Text design by Polar Design
Cover design by Linda Forss

Printed in China

Acknowledgements

Cover: Crocodiles bask in the sun on a riverbank. (Australian Picture Library © Oliver Strewe)

A.N.T. Photo Library, pp. 4, 29 © Silvestris, 6, 9 © Paddy Ryan, 7 © Dave Watts, 8, 10, 23 & 30, 28 © Michael Cermak, 13, 14, 16 & 30 © Frithfoto, 15 & 30 D. B. Carter, 17, 18 © Otto Rogge, 22, 24 © Nigel Dennis, 26 Kelvin Aitken, 27 © Sunset; Auscape, pp. 5 © Reg Morrison, 19 © Jim Frazier, 20 © Jan Aldenhoven, 25 & 30 D. Parer & E. Parer-Cook; Australian Picture Library, pp. 11 © Minden Picture, 12 © Oliver Strewe; Skyscans, Darwin, p. 21.

While every care has been taken to trace and acknowledge copyright, the publisher tenders their apologies for any accidental infringement where copyright has proved untraceable.

Contents

Life Cycles

All animals change as they live and grow. They begin life as tiny creatures. They become adults that will produce their own young. The crocodile has its own special life cycle.

Crocodiles Are Reptiles

Crocodiles belong to a group of animals called reptiles. A reptile's body is covered with **scales**. Its young hatch from eggs.

scales

Keeping Warm

Reptiles are cold-blooded animals. Their body temperature is as warm or as cold as the air or water around them. Crocodiles bask in the sunshine to warm themselves.

Keeping Cool

A crocodile cannot sweat when it is too hot. Instead, it cools off by opening its mouth or by lying in the water.

Food

Some crocodiles live in salt water. Others live in fresh water. Adult crocodiles eat fish, smaller crocodiles, and other animals.

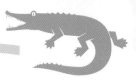

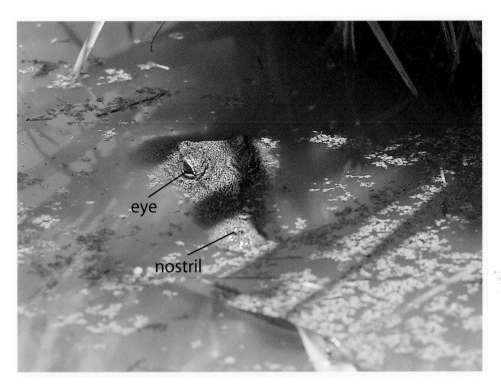

eye

nostril

A crocodile's nostrils are on the top of its snout. Its eyes are on the top of its head. It can hide its body underwater as it waits to **ambush** its prey. Crocodiles hunt large animals such as pigs, cattle, and horses.

Courting

Crocodiles are ready to **mate** when they are between 10 and 16 years old. Male and female crocodiles **court**. First, they call to each other by **bellowing**.

These crocodiles are courting.

Crocodile partners slap their heads in the water. They touch snouts and rub their necks together. They gently push each other under the water.

Mating

Crocodiles mate in the water. Most do not stay together after they have mated.

Building a Nest

The female crocodile is ready to lay her eggs about one month after mating. She chooses a place near the water to build her nest. Crocodiles make their nests at night.

Most crocodiles build nests from mud, grass, leaves, and sticks. The female carries these materials in her mouth.

Females build nests for their eggs.

This female is guarding her nest.

A nest is about 8 feet (2.5 meters) wide and
3 feet (1 meter) high. It can take as long as
one month to build a nest.

Laying Eggs

The female crocodile uses her back feet to make a hole in the nest. She lays her eggs in the hole at night. Then she covers them with grass and mud.

A female lays her eggs.

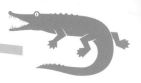

Crocodile eggs lie in a nest.

Crocodiles lay between 25 and 90 eggs.
Older crocodiles lay more eggs than
younger crocodiles.

Incubation

The nest is like a **compost** pile. It heats up as the grass and leaves rot.

nest

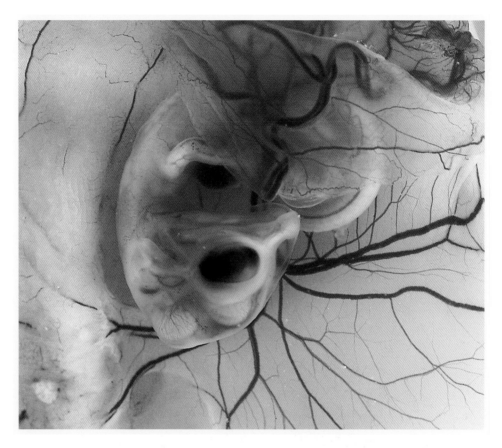

This baby crocodile is developing inside an egg.

The heat keeps the eggs warm as they develop. Crocodile eggs **incubate** for between 60 and 90 days.

Keeping Watch

The female crocodile digs a **wallow** close to her nest. She goes without food while she keeps watch over her eggs.

A female crocodile watches her eggs from a wallow.

Water monitors and other lizards eat crocodile eggs.

An animal might try to take the eggs. The crocodile leaves her wallow to chase it away. Lizards, birds, and snakes are some of the **predators** that raid crocodile nests.

Hatching

The young crocodiles are ready to hatch.
They call to their mother from inside their
shells. The mother crocodile hears them.
She digs down in the nest to find the eggs.

A young crocodile hatches from its egg.

egg tooth

Hatchlings have a special egg tooth on the end of their snouts. They use this hard point to help them break out of the egg.

The female crocodile sometimes uses
her teeth to help break open the eggs.
She carries the hatchlings to a pool near
the water.

A female carries a young crocodile in her mouth.

The Pod

At first the young crocodiles stay together in a family group called a pod.

Feeding

Young crocodiles stay close to their nest for about two years. At first they eat insects and tadpoles. They eat fish, birds, and small **mammals** as they grow older.

A young crocodile catches a dragonfly.

Predators

The mother crocodile protects her young from predators. Animals such as lizards, water birds, turtles, and larger crocodiles hunt for young crocodiles. Young crocodiles can also look after themselves. They have sharp teeth to chase off the predators.

A Dangerous Life

Young crocodiles are always in danger from predators. Half of all the hatchlings from a nest will die before they are 1 year old.

A Species in Danger

Crocodiles are in danger from people, too. Hunters used to kill crocodiles for their skins. Today many countries protect crocodiles so that they do not become **extinct**.

These handbags and shoes were made from crocodile and snake skins.

The Life Cycle of a Crocodile

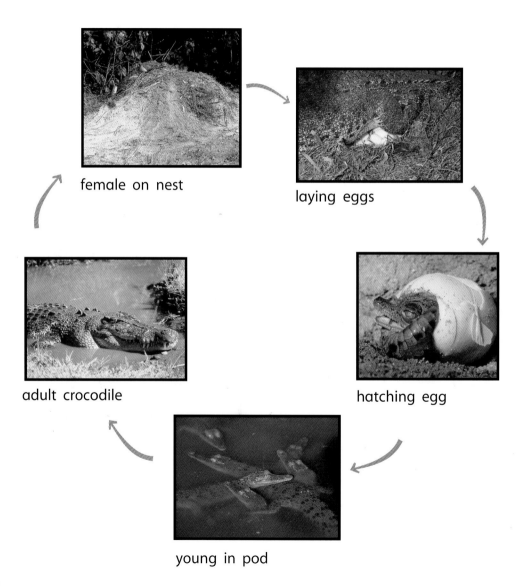

female on nest

laying eggs

adult crocodile

hatching egg

young in pod

Glossary

ambush   to attack unexpectedly

bellow   to roar loudly; crocodiles bellow to attract a mate.

compost   a mixture of rotted plants and manure that is added to soil to make it richer

court   to try to attract a mate

extinct   to no longer exist

hatchling   a young crocodile under 20 inches (50 centimeters) long

incubate   to keep an egg warm to help it develop

mammal   a warm-blooded animal that feeds its young with its own milk

mate   to join with a breeding partner to produce young

predator   an animal that hunts other animals for food

scales   thin, bony plates that protect the reptile's body

wallow   a shallow, muddy hole

Index